11/16/14

To Pre

Of all the miracles
God performs, the
most compelling is...

# The Miracle of You !

Vicki Andree

*Vicki Andree*

Ps 139:13-16

# Dedication

Trevor, Saraiah, and Vivienne

my grand miracles.

# Contents

# Bible Copyrights

# THE MIRACLE OF YOU

*"Men go abroad to wonder at the heights of mountains, at the huge waves of the sea, at the long courses of the rivers, at the vast compass of the ocean, at the circular motions of the stars, and they pass by themselves without wondering."—St. Augustine*

How many times have you looked at the stars and been overwhelmed with the thought that God created such a magnificent universe? How many times have you visited the seashore and, as you listened to the power behind the waves, wondered how a God that created the ocean could even see you ? How many times have you looked out your window at a tree and wondered at the creativity of God? Admit it; His creativity has taken your breath away more than once during your lifetime.

Our God is all about creativity. He loves everything He has created.

Mankind is God's most magnificent creation. Our physical capabilities alone are remarkable. We can do more than just walk upright. We can run marathons, we can lift weights, we can manipulate our hands and fingers, our bodies are amazing. But even more amazing is the spirit within us. When we feel like we can't possibly make another move physically, our spirit can kick in and make that impossible move and the next one, and the next one.

How many times have you looked at yourself and felt defeated, crushed or worthless? This devotional will help you see yourself as God created you to be, a magnificent creation, made in His image. Join me on this delightful journey through the Bible. As we study each verse, you will see—the miracle is you.

# 1: God Is With You Now

*"God said to Moses, 'I AM WHO I AM.' And*
*He said, 'Thus you shall say to the children of Israel,*
*I AM has sent me to you'" (Exodus 3:14 NKJV).*

That same God who created the universe spoke through the prophets to give messages to the people He created. This amazing God, that created the Milky Way, the mountains, and the seas, cared enough to communicate with us through gifted men and women who listened to Him.

Moses was tending his father-in-law's flock when he came upon a bush that seemed to be on fire. He saw that the bush didn't burn up, and continued to burn long after it should have been a pile of ashes. His curiosity led him to approach the bush. When the Lord saw that Moses had come over to look, He called to Moses from the bush. God told Moses to take off his shoes because he was standing on holy ground.

Then the Lord told Moses He was sending him to Pharaoh to bring His people out of Egypt. Moses went into immediate shock and denial. He basically said he couldn't do it and even if he tried, who would believe him? But God showed him that he could do it.

Moses wanted to know how to answer the people when they asked about this God who sent him. And that's when God identified Himself as "I AM." He assured Moses and the people that "HE IS" exactly what they need in their situation and "HE IS" with them now and always. "HE IS" on their side.

We as a people are so very special that God Himself, the Creator of the universe, not only sent Moses to free His people from captivity, but also identified Himself to us and the rest of the world. This is how He wants to be identified. "I AM." That means "HE IS" now. The miracle is that God is with you right now. .

# 2: You Are Salt And Light

*"You are the salt of the earth; but if the salt loses its flavor, how shall it be seasoned? It is then good for nothing but to be thrown out and trampled underfoot by men. You are the light of the world. A city that is set on a hill cannot be hidden" (Matt 5:13-14 NKJV).*

You are the salt of the earth. It's a phrase people use when they speak of someone's integrity. Someone who is the salt of the earth can be trusted. They are solid and considered the best and noblest elements of society. Here Jesus is saying that we are the ones who give flavor to life.

Salt was used as a preservative in ancient times. Even today you will find it used against bacteria, mold and spoiling. The way it works is that salt draws water out of cells via the process of osmosis. If you add enough salt, too much water will be removed from a cell for it to stay alive or reproduce. This keeps bacteria from living and growing in beef jerky.

Strangely, our body also needs salt in order to live. It is

both a flavoring and a necessity to maintain our body's chemical and electrical balance. Salt can be very useful or deadly.

Beyond that, salt creates thirst. One of the best things we can do as believers is create in others a thirst for more knowledge and relationship with Jesus. Let's be useful, not deadly!

You are also the light of the world. As a believer in Christ, you hold the light of eternity in your hands. You can share this light to bring others into the Kingdom. Add these to the positive qualities the Lord has poured out upon you. You are the salt of the earth and the light of the world shines through you. The miracle is you.

# 3:  You Are HIS Child

*"But as many as received Him, to them He gave the right to become children of God, to those who believe in His name" (John 1:12 NKJV).*

As far back as I can remember I knew Jesus existed. My family lived in a small town in Nebraska. We lived in a basement apartment with few extravagances. In fact, I remember my mother sewing cotton skirts for me to wear to school. On days when my sisters and I walked home in blizzards wearing our cotton skirts, we were frozen! My sisters and I shared the same bed until I was twelve years old. On cold nights we kept each other warm.

Poverty can have a debilitating effect on a child. Once in awhile my mother would send me to the store because she was fixing our favorite meal - goulash! We always looked forward to that day. As I said, she would send me to the store—for a quarter pound of hamburger. How my mother fed a family of five on a quarter pound of hamburger is a mystery to me. Nowadays one can hardly order a hamburger with less than a quarter pound of ground beef in it.

As children we used to say, we're poor in money, but we're rich in love. And to this day my siblings and I remain very close. Years later I realized how poor we were. We never got new clothes. We rode bicycles built from junkyard scraps. We made our own toys out of rocks and our imaginations. When things came up at school and our father couldn't buy them for us, we did feel poor, comparing ourselves to the other kids.

Then one day I realized just how rich I am. I received Him at a young age. And He gave me the RIGHT to become HIS CHILD! I am a child of God, the King, Creator of the universe! He's my Dad and He owns everything. So there. The miracle is that you are His child.

# 4: You can Abide In HIM

*"I am the vine, you are the branches. He who abides in Me, and I in him, bears much fruit; for without Me you can do nothing"* (John 15:5 NKJV).

The secret is abiding. He is the vine and we are indeed the branches. When we accept Him and seek His face continually, we can be incredibly fruitful. We can achieve things we never thought possible. We can climb impossible mountains, overcome impossible odds, and do it with little effort. As we lean on Him, He takes the burden.

When the Scripture says, "for without Me you can do nothing," it means that without Him you can do nothing that counts. Some things count for eternity. Other things count for today, but they may not last.

There's not going to be a Fortune 500 list in Heaven. Making money seems to be the focus of society these days. You heard the joke about the man who died and went to Heaven. St. Peter met him at the gate and asked him what he was trying to bring in. The man said he wanted to bring his gold with him. After some time, Peter shrugged and said the man could take it in. But since Heaven's streets are made of gold, it was as though the man carried in a load of concrete!

The Lord can give us beyond what we could ever think or imagine. It goes far beyond money or material possessions. Although, that can be part of the blessing. Abide in Him. Abide means live. Live in Him. He can and He will make your life more exciting and adventurous than ever, if you'll just trust Him. Be faithful and hang on tight! No matter what happens, you will be glorifying God and doing something that matters. The miracle is that you can abide in Him.

# 5: God Wants To Be Your Friend

*"No longer do I call you servants, for a servant does not know what his master is doing; but I have called you friends, for all things that I heard from My Father I have made known to you" (John 15:15 NKJV).*

Our Father is supernatural. While on Earth, Jesus was one hundred percent God and one hundred percent man. He was in constant contact with God. And this is the mystery of that relationship. Jesus is God.

Scripture reveals God's intention toward us is love. Jesus says that He will no longer call his disciples servants. As believers we fit into that small group called disciples. This is not just for the twelve; it is for us. He says a servant does not know what his master is doing. The Lord gave us the Scriptures, revealing His plan to the very end. We know His plan is for our good and benefits others. He says we are His friends because all things He heard from His Father He has made known to us. It's in the Bible. It takes two to form a friendship. Get to know Him by reading His thoughts and plans for us.

Friendship can never be one-sided. He will walk with us. He speaks to us through His word, through Church, and through His people. As we listen, He speaks to us personally through the Holy Spirit in our quiet times. "Be Still and know that I am God" (Psalm 46:10). He will walk along side of us when we feel completely alone. We can run to Him in times of trouble and He will defend us.

Our side of the friendship is to keep studying His Word, to pray without ceasing, and to fellowship with His other friends — other believers. We can do this by finding a Bible believing church. Spend some quiet time alone with Him. The miracle is that He wants to be your friend.

# 6: God Chose You

*"You did not choose Me, but I chose you and*
*appointed you to go and bear fruit — fruit that will*
*last. Then the Father will give you whatever you ask*
*in My name" (John 15:16 NIV).*

The God of the universe chose you. The same God who commanded the universe to be formed out of what was invisible chose you. Not only that, he appointed you to go and bear fruit. He appointed you to go out into the world and do good deeds in His name. He wants to use you to bring others into His kingdom. Now I must ask you something. What could be more exhilarating than to be working for the Lord God Almighty?

God isn't like other employers. He never gives you a job without giving you the tools to get the job done. You may think you have no idea how to work for God, but you would be wrong about that. And He is not interested in having you do anything that will not last throughout eternity. If that's hard to get your head around, don't feel alone. Most people in the world have no concept of eternity or working for the Lord God Almighty. This puts you in a very select group.

And yet, you are free to recruit others to join in furthering the Kingdom of God. Jesus said that we could ask the Father for anything in His name and receive it. The context is important. He means anything that will help you get the job done. Yes, the job of bringing another soul into the Kingdom. Keep in mind, God works in mysterious ways. He chose you, didn't He? You may be like Moses and say that you can't do it. If you say that, you would be wrong. Moses succeeded and so will you. God will bring you to the place where it will be your greatest desire to help others into His Kingdom. The miracle is that He chose you.

# 7:  You Have Been Set Free

*"But now having been set free from sin, and having become slaves of God, you have your fruit to holiness, and the end, everlasting life" (Romans 6:22 NKJV).*

You may not realize that you have lived a life of imprisonment! Paul writes in Romans about how being slaves to sin has no future. Sinning day after day desensitizes the mind. Soon it seems all right to go after our worldly desires constantly with no thought as to the future. This is what the evil one loves. He rejoices. Yes! Satisfy your immediate needs and do not think about what the God who created you desires for you.

If we stop to think about what we are doing, we see the folly of our ways. Paul goes on to say something I find very interesting. He says that when we were slaves to sin we were free from the control of righteousness. Then he asks the defining question. "What benefit did you reap at that time from the things you are now ashamed of? Those things result in death!"

I like the way Eugene Peterson writes it in The Message.

"Recall...at one time the more you did just what you felt like doing — not caring about others, not caring about God — the worse your life became and the less freedom you had? And how much different it is now as you live in God's freedom, your lives healed and expansive in holiness?"

Then Peterson quotes Paul as saying "As long as you did what you felt like doing, ignoring God, you didn't have to bother with right thinking or right living, or anything for that matter. But do you call that a free life? What did you get out of it? Nothing you're proud of now. Where did it get you? A dead end."

Jesus freed us to enjoy everlasting life. Now we can now be free in the pleasure of paying attention to what God tells us. The miracle is that freedom in Christ is freedom indeed! He has freed us! We no longer have to strive for our own glory. We can relax and bask in His glory.

# 8: God's Spirit Leads You

*"For as many as are led by the Spirit of God, these*
*are sons of God" (Romans 8:14 NKJV).*

We are children of God. Now that we have accepted the freedom offered by God, we can be led by the Holy Spirit. When we accept Jesus into our hearts, we are sealed with the Holy Spirit. We can now kiss that old sin-life good-bye.

What a relief to focus on the things of God rather than on the things of this world! And God has things for us to do. It can be a very exciting time as God begins to reveal His plan for each of us. We begin to live on a higher level.

We learn over time to be led by the Spirit. In fact, I believe much more than we can know happens to us when we receive the Holy Spirit. When we receive the Holy Spirit, we change. We are given gifts (skills). We begin to think and act differently. We become citizens of Heaven, making us aliens here on Earth. It's the part of His image that we are made in, and, you can laugh if you want to, but I believe that some day scientists may find that our DNA changes.

Everything we learn about God in the Bible is astounding. He is so beyond what we can fathom. What He has revealed to us in His Word is but a fraction of Him. We couldn't handle all of it now. Seriously, look at that universe again. We cannot even count the stars, yet He knows each one of them by name. And focusing back on ourselves, He knows the numbers of hairs on our heads. That is quite a feat, because mine change every time I take a shower.

The miracle is, that as a son or daughter of God, you are led by His Spirit.

# 9: You Are Adopted

*"For you did not receive the spirit of bondage again to
fear, but you received the Spirit of adoption by whom
we cry out, 'Abba, Father.' The Spirit Himself bears
witness with our spirit that we are children of God"
(Romans 8:15-16 NKJV).*

In the Hebrew 'Abba' is the expression of a very close
relationship. It's as close as a little child crying out to his
father saying, "Daddy!" It's the word Jesus used when He
prayed to His Father in Heaven. And Jesus had the right to
call God, Abba, because He trusted His Father.

Here's the amazing miracle. Instead of human beings
needing to fear a just God for all of our lives, He found a
way to reach down and adopt us through our faith in
Christ. This is what I leaned on as a child from a poor
family, living what could have been a very sad life. At times
I reveled in my position as a child of God. I had been
taught that I was loved as much as John, Paul, or any of the
apostles. My spirit would soar with happiness as I looked at
the blue sky and imagined my Heavenly Father looking
down on me with love and approval in His eyes.

"Ah," you might say, "the innocence of a child." However, even today I find the knowledge of His Fatherhood very comforting. Many times I have cried out to Him, Abba, Father! Instantly I feel His presence.

Being an adult certainly does not exempt you from being adopted by God. My husband was adopted as an adult. God's in the business of adopting all ages, colors, and sizes of people. He's got enough love for all of us. And the very best part of being adopted by God is that He has no special favorites. Every one of His children are favored.

The miracle here is that, by the Holy Spirit, we can have that same intimate relationship with God that Jesus had with Him. And just like Jesus, we can have it for eternity!

# 10: You Are Joint Heirs

*"Now if we are children, then we are heirs — heirs of God and co-heirs with Christ, if indeed we share in His sufferings in order that we may also share in His glory" (Romans 8:17 NIV).*

Can you imagine what a child of God inherits? As a child I could only think of all the riches I was going to inherit. I could have my very own room, my very own house, my very own town! The kids at school wouldn't make fun of me any more because I would be super rich!

Then I found out all of it was going to burn to ashes in the end times. So what will be left? Money and iPhones won't matter. Our inheritance will be so much greater. We get new bodies. We get power. We will see things clearly and finally understand. We will sing with the angels. And much, much more.

As Christians in the United States today, we are suffering on several different levels. In recent years corporations have made it against policy for an employee to discuss religion. It seems this is directed more at Christians than other religions because one could lose their job for mentioning Jesus. Rather than having the freedom to speak about our Lord, we are threatened if we do.

Teachers are not allowed to pray in our schools. We are not allowed to pray at government functions, and I heard that the military has told Chaplains that they could not pray in Jesus' name. We endure this persecution, knowing that one day we will be glorified with our Lord and King, Jesus Christ.

The miracle is that we can share in everything Jesus will inherit.

# 11: The Spirit of God Is In You

*"Do you not know that you are the temple of God and that the Spirit of God dwells in you" (1 Corinthians 3:16 NKJV)?*

He is with us every day. Who else can be at our side through it all? He shares the good times and the bad times. He dwells in us. Perhaps we should stop and think about that for a minute.

The Holy Spirit lives inside of us. He is that unconquerable Spirit within us. He gives us strength when we feel like we can't go on. He comforts us when we are in pain. And He goes with us where ever we go. I remember standing in front of the door of a place I frequented. Suddenly I felt tug at my conscience. What's that? I've been here many times and now I got a red flag. I left and have never returned. I have no desire to return.

Something like this may have happened to you at some time. I hope you listened. When you drag the Holy Spirit some place He doesn't want to go, His voice could become quieter and the sounds of the world louder.

If I'm the temple that houses the Holy Spirit, the Spirit that was sent to me by Jesus to comfort and protect me, then I should be as holy as I can be. The fact that He wants to live in me is extremely humbling. This God, this universe-maker, this all powerful God, has put His seal on me. First He breathed life into me on the day I was born, and then he came to live in me on the day I was born again. This is a miracle.

# 12: You Are Not Your Own

*"Do you not know that your body is a temple of the Holy Spirit, who is in you, whom you have from God? You are not your own; you were bought at a price. Therefore honor God with your body" (1 Corinthians 6:19,20 NIV).*

You were bought at a price. What an understatement. The price Jesus paid began before His birth here on Earth. He knew before His birth that His very purpose for coming to Earth was to save us from sin. He was born in a stable. The conditions of His birth were humbling.

He was a toddler when Mary and Joseph took Him and fled to Egypt for safety. He was mocked as a child and called illegitimate. He endured bullying and disrespect in his hometown. Before He started His ministry here on Earth, He went to his cousin, John the Baptist. There He was baptized, and His Father in Heaven spoke. "You are my Son, Whom I love; with You I am well pleased."

As soon as Jesus returned from the Jordan He submitted to forty days of temptation in the wilderness. All the time

He had you in mind. He could have stopped any of it at any time, but He didn't. He had you in mind and He knew what He had to do.

He overcame temptation and began His ministry after choosing twelve men to teach the ways of God. Then He took them with Him as He taught the masses, healed the sick and bound the brokenhearted.

Then He went through what we call Holy Week. It doesn't seem very holy to me. He was betrayed. He was arrested on false charges in the middle of the night. He submitted to an illegal trial. He was beaten to an unrecognizable bloody pulp. Then they nailed Him to a cross. No, you are not your own. You were bought at a price. How valuable you are to Him! This is the miracle. And yes, you owe Him.

# 13: You Are The Body Of Christ

*"Now you are the body of Christ, and each one of you is a part of it" (1 Corinthians 12:27 NIV).*

The body of Christ is not limited to certain church denominations or religions. Remember, Christ is not about religion. Each believer is a part of the body of Christ. He is about a personal relationship with Him. Any one who has accepted Jesus as Lord and Savior is a member of the body of Christ.

There are many members in the body of Christ and as stated above, each one of you is a part of it. That means you have a specific role in the body just as a church or denomination has a specific role. Your role is more than going to church and sitting in a pew each Sunday. Although, going to church is an important activity for any member of the body of Christ.

God has gifted you. Everyone has at least one gift. You should know what your gifts are; what things come naturally to you. If you don't, find out what they are because He has given them to you for a reason.

God can use anything. If you have a gift for talking, then pray, study, and find out everything you can about Him and talk about it. If your gift is walking, then pray, study and find out everything you can about Him and walk it around the neighborhood. Jesus walked everywhere, and when He did, He spoke of the prophets and the days to come.

If your gift is criticizing, then pray, study, and realize that this gift is not from God. Ask God for the gift of encouragement and He will replace the devil's gift with His. Pray and ask God how to use your particular gift. There is no finer, no more exciting adventure, than to be in the act of working for God.

He has allowed us to be His hands and feet here on Earth. This is a miracle; the God who created the universe trusts you enough to speak for Him.

# 14: He Gives You Another Chance

*"But because God was so gracious, so very generous, here I am. And I'm not about to let His grace go to waste. Haven't I worked hard trying to do more than any of the others? Even then, my work didn't amount to all that much. It was God giving me the work to do, God giving me the energy to do it. So whether you heard it from me or those others, it's all the same. We spoke God's truth and you entrusted your lives." (1 Corinthians 15:10-11 The Message).*

Earlier Paul tried to stamp out Christianity. He was the least likely person for God to use to further the Kingdom. Paul went around persecuting Christians in any way he could. He stood in the crowd when Stephen was stoned. Perhaps he was moved when Stephen's last words were, "Lord Jesus, receive my spirit. Lord, do not hold this sin against them."

It wasn't long after that the Lord appeared to Paul. Christianity could no longer be denied. He had seen Christ. Now he was doing the same thing that Stephen had done, serving the Lord. If God had acted without grace, you can be sure that Paul would have been subject to a miserable life and most likely, a horrible death. After all, Paul was an enemy of the faith.

And yet, the God who created the universe reached out to Paul. God made Paul's life one that Christians strive to emulate. He dedicated the rest of his life to preaching the gospel. He preached to his Jewish colleagues and they wanted to kill him. He was beaten, stoned, shipwrecked, and more...all in the service to the One who extended the hand of grace.

And the miracle is this: God loves you so much that He will forgive you and give you another chance at life. He can change you, and He will. All we need do is lean on Him.

# 15:  You Are Reconciled

*"All this is from God, who reconciled us to Himself*
*through Christ and gave us the ministry of*
*reconciliation: that God was reconciling the world to*
*Himself in Christ, not counting men's sins against*
*them. And He has committed to us the message of*
*reconciliation" (2 Corinthians 5:18-19 NIV).*

As long as we were bound to this world by sin, we could not have a relationship with our Holy God. For this reason, God sent Jesus. Someone had to pay the price for the sins of the world. Since Jesus willingly gave Himself to pay that price, we now have the humble honor to have a relationship with God through Christ. We ought to feel humbled to the very core of our existence that we can pray and know that God hears our prayers.

In addition God has committed to us the message of reconciliation. In other words, we are privileged, and beyond that—obligated to share this good news throughout the world.

False religions demand that their followers do

extraordinary good deeds, live exemplary lives, give substantial monetary gifts, and follow difficult traditions. This is all required for the person to advance to a higher level.

Trying to work your way to Heaven is futile. God reached down to provide a way for us. He provided a sinless man to take on our sin and be the sacrifice for all who believe. When we accept Christ, we throw ourselves on His mercy. We cannot do enough good deeds or give enough money to cover our sins. It is impossible. But with God all things are possible. He did it all. He paid the price and we became His children. Sharing His story, telling about this reconciliation, is the best thing you could do for another person. The miracle is that God handed the torch to you. Run with it!

# 16: You Are God's Child

*"For you are all sons of God through faith in Christ Jesus" (Galatians 3:26 NKJV).*

You are God's child through your solid faith in Jesus. Now what do you do? How do you live the faith life? There cannot be a simple answer for this, and yet there can be. You pray—lots! You study the Scriptures, His love letter to you. You never forsake Him. You never deny Him. Sometimes you might defend Him, even though He doesn't need defending. He is very capable of taking care of Himself. Defending His Word is another matter.

One of my colleagues at the office suddenly broke out swearing, using the name of Jesus to express his frustration at his computer. He saw me standing there and stopped.

His face reddened and he said, "Oh, I'm so sorry."

I must admit that I was offended, but I wasn't about to let him off so easily. So I said to him, "I'm not the one you offended. Take it up with Him."

As a child of God I cannot help but be offended when someone uses Jesus' name to swear. It happens more and more these days. My purpose in responding the way I did was to get the man to stop and think about what he had done. I don't want people to talk about my Father that way. I asked the Holy Spirit to take care of it.

When Jesus was arrested in the Garden of Gethsemane, Peter drew his sword and fought for Jesus. Jesus stopped him. Usually God doesn't want us to start a fight for Him. But I think He want us to always be willing to defend His name.

Here's the miracle. God is your Father. He will grant you the wisdom and humility to know when a teachable moment has presented itself.

# 17: You Can Be Like Jesus

*"For as many of you as were baptized into Christ*
*have put on Christ" (Galatians 3:27 NKJV).*

The Message says it this way: "But now you have arrived at
your destination: by faith in Christ you are in direct
relationship with God. Your baptism in Christ was not just
washing you up for a fresh start. It also involved dressing
you in an adult faith wardrobe—Christ's life, the fulfillment
of God's original promise."

Wearing an adult faith wardrobe doesn't have much to
do with clothing. It's our spiritual wardrobe that needs
examining. We have a new way of looking at things. Putting
on Christ is our effort to be more like Him. The more we
learn about Him, the more we understand what to put on
and what to take off.

One thing that may have to change is the way you talk.
Words are powerful and should always be used in an
edifying way. Forget the coarse language and jokes that we
used to listen to. We're putting Holiness on and there's no
room for profanity or gossip. Read the words in red in your

Bible and begin to speak like Jesus does, comforting, direct, honest. He never minced words and neither should we. This may be a new thing, but we can learn it.

Put on compassion. Stop and listen when people talk. Are they asking for your help? Do they need Jesus? Take time to listen. Put on gratefulness. We must be thankful for all He has done for us. Put on humility, Micah 6:8 gives us a clue: "He has showed you, O man, what is good. And what does the Lord require of you? To act justly and to love mercy and to walk humbly with your God." And the miracle is that you have been given these garments. You can be encouraging, compassionate, and humble.

# 18: You Are One In Christ Jesus

*"There is neither Jew nor Greek, there is neither slave
nor free, there is neither male nor female; for you are
all one in Christ Jesus" (Galatians 3:28 NKJV).*

Thomas Jefferson wrote, "We hold these truths to be self-evident: that all men are created equal; that they are endowed by their Creator with certain unalienable rights; that among these are life, liberty, and the pursuit of happiness..."

Equality. It's a conundrum in our world. Our Governments enacts laws to insure that everyone is treated equally. It seems to be what everybody wants. In 1870 the right to vote was expanded to include all races. It wasn't until 1920 that women were given that right. Evidently, it takes some time for equality to kick in, even with the government.

Erich Fromm, got close to defining equality when he said, "We are all alike, on the inside." Of course, one would think a psychoanalyst like Fromm would know that is definitely not true. People can be very different on the inside.

Mark Twain (1835-1910) said it this way. "All people are equal, it is not birth, it is virtue alone that makes the difference." I would ask Mark Twain how he could make such a convoluted statement. If virtue makes the difference, then they are not equal.

The truest quote I found was in an ageless proverb, announcing the stark truth. "Six feet of earth make all men equal." That is all the world can offer.

We are all one in Christ Jesus. It is our faith in Christ that surpasses Jew, Greek, slave or free, male or female. If we are in Christ, we are all equal heirs. When we approach His throne, all of us must be on bended knee. We are equal because the same Holy Spirit is in each of us. As the apostle John learned when he asked for a special place in Heaven, Jesus has no need to show favoritism.

The miracle is that He has an unlimited supply of love. He loves each of His kids totally, completely, and without limits all the time. You never have to wait your turn. Your time is now.

# 19:  Jesus is Your Brother

*"But when the time arrived that was set by God the Father, God sent His Son, born among us of a woman, born under the conditions of the law so that He might redeem those of us who have been kidnapped by the law. Thus we have been set free to experience our rightful heritage. You can tell for sure that you are now fully adopted as His own children because God sent the Spirit of His Son into our lives crying out, 'Papa! Father!' Doesn't that privilege of intimate conversation with God make it plain that you are not a slave, but a child? And if you are a child, you're also an heir, with complete access to the inheritance"* (Galatians 4:4-7 The Message).

You understand that God planned all of this before you were in the womb. He chose the time that Christ would come to free us from the law of sin and death. He chose the day that Christ would be raised up to show the world that He overcame death. He chose the day that Christ left this Earth and ascended into Heaven. And He chose the day you were born.

The only problem is, you were born into slavery. Slavery to sin. So then He put circumstances in your life that eventually drew you to Him. He was with you through every valley. He was there for every mountain you've climbed. He used all of it to make you into the person you are today.

On the day you chose Christ, He opened His arms wide and pulled You into Him and Him into You. As soon as you chose Christ, you became sealed with the Holy Spirit. You became His adopted child. Our Heavenly Father is a gracious Father and a generous Father. The miracle is that you can call Jesus your brother. And if he is your brother, you also have complete access to the Father. Now is the time to enjoy that access.

# 20: God Made You An Heir

*"So you are no longer a slave, but a son; and since you are a son, God has made you also an heir" (Galatians 4:7 NIV).*

It's about time we talked about that inheritance. Just what is this inheritance? And how will we ever get our hands on it if God the Father never dies? That's the beauty of our supernatural God. Our Father doesn't have to die for us to receive the inheritance. In fact, we get some of our inheritance right away.

We inherit eternal life and the Holy Spirit within us. This we receive the moment we accept Jesus Christ into our hearts. Throughout the Bible we are promised many things, but the most valuable is what we got the moment we committed to Him. We have been delivered from the power of darkness and translated into the Kingdom where we stand redeemed and forgiven (Colossians 1:12-14). Through faith we can have all our needs supplied (Philippians 4:9). We can claim God's peace now (Philippians 4:7). We are more than conquerors because nothing can separate us from God's love (Romans 8:35-38).

We are promised that we will reign with Jesus from mansions in the Heavens. There will be no more death or mourning or crying or pain for the old order of things has passed away. We will live with other believers surrounded by the glory and love of God forever. Revelation 21:7 says, "He who overcomes will inherit all this, and I will be his God and he will be My Son."

The miracle is this: when this momentary life on Earth is over, you get to see God. You will actually see the invisible God. I believe the greatest piece of this great inheritance will be living with God in Heaven. Just the idea of seeing Him face to face every day is so very exciting and yet, immensely humbling.

# 21:  You Are A Saint

*"Paul, an apostle of Jesus Christ by the will of God,
To the saints in Ephesus, the faithful in Christ Jesus:
Grace and peace to you from God our Father and the
Lord Jesus Christ" (Ephesians 1:1-2 NIV).*

The apostle Paul refers to his fellow believers as saints. We think of saints as ones who have attained perfection. Most of us have been taught that a saint is someone who is dead, whose life conformed to Church teaching and who performed miracles before or after dying. You might think that you don't qualify to be a saint, or perhaps you do. I certainly know I wouldn't qualify. Paul had a different definition of saint.

The Bible actually teaches that the word 'saint' means one who is sanctified, or set apart for God. It is not a statement of a spiritual status that only a few Christians could ever attain. A saint is anyone who has a living relationship with God through His mercy and grace expressed in the death of the Lord Jesus Christ. Because of this definition, every Christian is a saint.

You are a saint. Being a saint is not just a title you earn. No need to go look in the mirror, your halo is not showing! Being a saint is a statement of your relationship with God through the Lord Jesus Christ. I would like to share one of many Scriptures that talk about saints. Luke mentioned saints in Acts 9:13, when Ananias spoke about Paul, saying, "I have heard many reports about this man and all the harm he has done to your saints in Jerusalem."

A saint can be a spiritual giant or a believer who struggles with their faith. A doctor, lawyer, housewife, mental patient, gongfermor, or anyone in any country that has a personal relationship with Jesus Christ. And that is a miracle! And as Paul reminds us, being a saint grants us grace and peace. Thank You, Lord.

# 22:  You Are Part Of His Body

*"No one abuses his own body, does he? No, he feeds
and pampers it. That's how Christ treats us, the
church, since we are part of His body. And this is why
a man leaves father and mother and cherishes his wife.
No longer two, they become "one flesh. This is a huge
mystery, and I don't pretend to understand it all.
What is clearest to me is the way Christ treats the
church. And this provides a good picture of how each
husband is to treat his wife, loving himself in loving
her, and how each wife is to honor her husband"
(Ephesians 5:29-33 The Message).*

Being part of the body of Christ brings up an obvious
question. What part of the body am I? This Scripture will
help to clarify what it means to be part of the body of
Christ. "For just as the body is one and has many members,
and all the members of the body, though many, are one
body, so it is with Christ. For in one Spirit we were all
baptized into one body—Jews or Greeks, slaves or free—
and all were made to drink of one Spirit. For the body does
not consist of one member but of many. If the foot should
say, "Because I am not a hand, I do not belong to the

body," that would not make it any less a part of the body. And if the ear should say, "Because I am not an eye, I do not belong to the body," that would not make it any less a part of the body" (1 Corinthians 12:12-16 ESV).

In Ephesians, Chapter five, Paul is reminding us how to live out our family relationships. Sometimes it takes all of the fruit of the Spirit to do it. The fruit of the Spirit is listed in Galatians 5:22, it is love, joy, peace, patience, goodness, kindness, gentleness, faithfulness and self control. We receive all of these when we get the Holy Spirit.

It's like having nine different boxes, each with a locked lid. Figuring out how to unlock it, get access to the fruit, and learning how to use it, is going to take time and practice. The key is prayer and submission.

Every part of the Body of Christ is about serving others. The miracle is that you can think of others as more important than yourself. You can practice this with your family.

## 23:  You Are Seated With Christ in Heaven

*"And God raised us up with Christ and seated us
with Him in the heavenly realms in Christ Jesus, in
order that in the coming ages He might show the
incomparable riches of His grace, expressed in His
kindness to us in Christ Jesus" (Ephesians 2:6-7
NIV).*

How can I be in Heaven and on Earth at the same time?
First of all, understand that this can only happen after you
are saved. You must have that person relationship with
Jesus before He's taking you to Heaven to be seated with
Him.

When you accepted Christ, you became completely and
eternally united with Christ. Jesus Christ is our Intercessor
and He is in constant communication with the Father.
When the Father looks at you, He sees Jesus Christ.
Remember when you were baptized? You were
ceremoniously buried in the water and then resurrected.
Beyond that, you ascended with Christ and were seated in
the heavenly realms. You and I are now a part of Christ. He
is in us and we are in Him. Jesus is seated at the right hand

of God.

Lift up His name and praise Him! He found a way to save us, and not only that, by His Spirit we are seated at the right hand of God. If Jesus is sitting at the right hand of God, we are right there with Him.

And guess what? We don't have to be nervous or afraid to be there because all of the things that would make us feel unworthy have been conquered by Jesus Christ on the cross. No, we shouldn't feel like we have the right to be there. We should feel gratitude for a loving God and a Savior, Jesus Christ. And this is truly a miracle—we can sit at the right hand of God and gaze at Him with awe and reverence.

# 24: You Are His Workmanship

*"For we are His workmanship, created in Christ Jesus for good works, which God prepared beforehand that we should walk in them" (Ephesians 2:10 NKJV).*

When I think of God's workmanship, I have to look at the things all around me. He created all the stars in the heavens. Every time I look up into a star studded night sky, my whole being soars with delight and wonder. Twinkling lights against a sapphire sky can take my breath away!

God is all about creativity. I look at the Rocky Mountains and try to understand the grandeur of the artist. I can't help but think if Him. The majesty of the front range doesn't begin to compare to Him. And, I am always astonished at the way He changes the appearance of those mountains every day. Every day the shadow of the clouds, the snow on the continental divide, the rain, or some other natural phenomena changes the look.

At the seashore I feel His power with each wave that washes up. God does not create ordinary things. He is supernatural. That, added to His creative genius (which is more than we could ever get our heads around) makes His creations both amazing and inspiring.

Our minds, bodies, and souls are made by a creative God Who didn't spare the energy or creativity it took to make us. We are amazing in so many ways. Did you know that our noses can remember fifty thousand different scents? And that's just our nose! The human eye and distinguish about ten million different colors.

In a lifetime, your brain's long-term memory can hold as many as one quadrillion (that's one million billion) separate bits of information. Now THAT'S a miracle!

# 25: You Are A Member Of God's Household

*"You're no longer wandering exiles. This Kingdom of
faith is now your home country. You're no longer
strangers or outsiders. You belong here, with as much
right to the name Christian as anyone. God is
building a home. He's using us all—irrespective of
how we got here—in what He is building. He used
the apostles and prophets for the foundation. Now
He's using you, fitting you brick by brick, stone by
stone, with Christ Jesus as the cornerstone that holds
all the parts together. We see it taking shape day after
day—a holy temple built by God, all of us built into
it, a temple in which God is quite at home"*
*(Ephesians 2:19-22 The Message).*

Imagine a field littered with individual bricks. Do you see a
building or do see a mess? So it is with Christians. Until we
are bonded with other Christians we are not yet part of the
Church. Jesus sees us as we can be, but the vision is not
reality until the work is done.

With Jesus as the cornerstone, He controls the shape
and form of the Church. He also controls the identification

of the Church. We are the building bricks of this ever growing temple of God. New bricks must be added. All the bricks must spiritually mature and grow into a holy temple in the Lord. We grow and mature in the community of the church with the bricks around us.

As God's people we must encourage those around us, be active in discipleship, and unashamedly stand against destructive activities. The Holy Spirit is the Supreme Builder of the Church because He is the supreme witness to Jesus Christ.

The miracle is that God can make something beautiful and holy out of a bunch of independent sinners. His temple is not complete until you are cemented into the place He reserved for you.

# 26: You Can Be Holy

*"You were taught with regard to your former way of life, to put off your old self, which is being corrupted by its deceitful desires; to be made new in the attitude of your minds; and to put on the new self, created to be like God in true righteousness and holiness"*
*(Ephesians 4:22-24 NIV).*

Many years ago there was a book, I'm OK—You're OK. But I was not OK. I was selfish and no amount of chanting positive affirmations could change that. Because the truth is, being selfish is not OK. Nobody wants "he was selfish" written on his tombstone.

The instant I became a Christian something did change. I received the Holy Spirit who daily encourages me to give up my old selfish ways and to consider others more important than myself. For awhile I didn't listen, but the Holy Spirit never gives up. As I read the Bible and listened to Christian music, I experienced a renewing of my mind.

Every battle begins in the mind. It's important to realize that fact, because many times we disregard our thought life when seeking change. We try change appearances and even the way we talk. However, the way we think is of greatest importance. Otherwise we fall back into the old habits.

Remember at the last supper when Jesus washed Peter's feet (John 13:10)? Jesus told Peter "you are clean though not every one of you. For He knew Judas was going to betray Him, and that' why He said not every one was clean. Even though Jesus knew that Peter would later deny Him, that behavior didn't make him unclean. Over time, through the work of the Holy Spirit, Peter's behavior did change.

The miracle is that I didn't become holy by behaving righteously, being holy means being set apart by God and that happened when I became a Christian. You are holy, and through the work of the Holy Spirit your behavior will change.

# 27:  You Are Getting A New Body

*"But there is far more to life for us. We're citizens of high Heaven! We're waiting the arrival of the Savior, Jesus Christ, who will transforms our earthly bodies into glorious bodies like His own. He'll make us beautiful and whole with the same powerful skill by which He is putting everything as it should be, under and around Him"* (Philippians 3:20 The Message).

I woke up this morning with a bit of a headache. I looked in the mirror and groaned. I needed to get in my office and get a couple of devotions finished before my girls came to visit. It took all I could do just to get myself into my office. My thinking was fuzzy with fierce ringing in my ears, a condition I ignored for years but am finally addressing.

Last night my husband and I had gone out for a quick bite to eat at a new restaurant near our home. It was Mexican food. I love Mexican food, but it is so much better with a Diet Pepsi. So, in spite of my caffeine intolerance, I ordered a Diet Pepsi. By the time we finished our meal, I was feeling a bit edgy.

On the way home we stopped to for a quick 'hello' at a friend's home. We enjoyed our visit and stayed much longer than intended. It was past bedtime (9:00 for me) when we got home. I was so tired, but we got interested in a project, and before we knew it, it was 11:00. We finally got to bed and David fell asleep. My Diet Pepsi caffeine indiscretion kept me awake for the next hour or more.

Praise God! He is going to give us new bodies, ones that are like His resurrected body. One that has not been corrupted by our own bad decisions such as not eating right, ageing, or even injuries. We will not need glasses or caffeine. It will be a glorious body built for eternity. For eternity. And this is a miracle.

# 28: You've Received Grace

*"To the saints and faithful brethren in Christ who are in Colosse: Grace to you and peace from God our Father and the Lord Jesus Christ" (Colossians 1:2 NKJV).*

Grace is my favorite word. In fact, I am working on a book right now that will be titled Grace. This simple salutation that Paul writes to the Colossians is filled with power and assurance. Grace and peace to you from God our Father and the Lord Jesus Christ.

Grace has been explained to me by an acronym. G-God's; R-Riches; A-at; C-Christ's; E-Expense. GRACE. I can't think of a better way to describe grace. God sent Christ to pay the debt of our sin, making us acceptable to have a relationship with God. God pours out blessings upon us every day. Did you see the sunrise this morning? Many times that is the first blessing of the day, but from there it just continues.

Did you get a good breakfast? Perhaps you met a friend and had a cup of tea. Perhaps you grabbed an Egg

McMuffin on the way to work. You got nourishment. You have a job. Perhaps you were out of gas and barely made it to the gas station, by the grace of God. Blessings. Grace.

God has shown us grace in a million different ways every day. The most beautiful thing about grace is that we can extend it to others. Yes, we can give grace. It's one of the things we do to be more like Christ. A friend said something that hurt you. Let grace cleanse that wound. When someone wants to cut in on you in traffic — let them in. My husband loves to say, "Why don't you be first?" when people do this to him. He means it. He explains that he has enough patience to arrive two seconds later if it makes someone happy. There's no room for resentment with grace. Grace is free for us, and free for us to give. That's the miracle. By receiving His grace, and bestowing grace to those around us, we are more like Christ.

# 29:  You Are With Christ

*"Your old life is dead. Your new life, which is your real life— even though invisible to spectators—is with Christ in God. He is your life. When Christ (your real life, remember) shows up again on this earth, you'll show up, too—the real you, the glorious you. Meanwhile, be content with obscurity, like Christ"*
*(Colossians 3:3-4 The Message).*

The Bible goes on to say that since the old life is dead we should put away the old things we used to do, knowing all the time it was wrong. Whatever we thought was more important than God falls into that category. Some of the things listed are sexual immorality, impurity, lust, evil, desires and greed. All of these are idolatry. And we need to let go of things like anger, rage, malice, slander, lying and filthy language.

What are we to do? If we let go of all these things, what will we replace them with? God has the answer to that question. Let me paraphrase what He has outlined for us in Colossians verse 12. First He says since we are His chosen people that we are dear to Him and loved. And because of that we can show compassion, kindness, humility, gentleness and patience to others.

He wants us to be considerate of each other and to forgive each other. Don't ever forget how Christ forgave you. Then He says the neatest thing ever in verse 14, "And over all these virtues put on love, which binds them all together in perfect unity" (NIV).

We don't earn our salvation by doing all the right things. Jesus did all the right things and in fact, He did everything needed for our salvation. All we have to do is accept that gift. Beyond that, He gives us the power to do all the things talked about above. And the miracle is that you are with Christ now—.

# 30:  You're Elected!

*"...knowing, beloved brethren, your election by God"*
*(1 Thessalonians 1:4 NKJV).*

Election by God! If we were talking politics here, with someone like God backing you there would be no doubt as to who would win. We are not talking politics, but we are talking about winners. Election is another one of those blessings we receive by grace.

Another word for election is 'chosen.' In Matthew 22:14 Jesus tells a story about a Wedding Feast. The purpose of the story is to explain the phrase "many are called but few are chosen." The story begins with the king sending servants out to invite guests to the feast. Sadly, those invited didn't come because they either didn't like the king or they had more important things to do.

Then the king told the servants to invite anybody to come and they filled the wedding hall with all kinds of people. The king sees a man not wearing the proper wedding attire and sends him away. Jesus tells us the point of the story. He says that many are called, but few are chosen. Only those who are covered by the blood of Christ, only those who have been 'chosen' will be welcomed into the Kingdom of God.

Election is being chosen by God through the Holy Spirit. He draws us to Him and we have the choice to accept the covering of the blood of Christ or to reject it. He gave us free will and sometimes that free will imprisons more than frees us. But still, the choice is ours. The miracle is that when we accept, we are elected. The blood of Christ cleanses us and makes us presentable.

# 31: You Are Light

*"You're sons of Light, daughters of Day. We live under wide open skies and know where we stand. So let's not sleepwalk through life like those others. Let's keep our eyes open and be smart. People sleep at night and get drunk at night. But not us! Since we're creatures of Day, let's act like it. Walk out into the daylight sober, dressed up in faith, love, and the hope of salvation" (1 Thessalonians 5:4-8, The Message).*

We should be celebrating every day! Jesus provides freedom far beyond what we could ever dream. When I first accepted Christ as my Lord and Savior, I didn't have a clue as to what I was getting into. I smile here. I only knew that I wanted Jesus in my life. I had no idea that He would make my life better, more interesting and more exciting than I could have imagined at that time.

Even after my salvation I lay dormant for years, not using all the opportunities He laid before me. I never felt worthy to serve as the light He intended me to be. I allowed the evil one to whisper sweet nothings in my ear. There's nothing you can do for Jesus; He doesn't need you.

You would put Him to shame, so just stay back and keep your mouth shut. Oh, you see someone hurting? You don't need to help, just pray. Yes, even the devil will tell you to pray if it keeps you from being a light.

We have hope and a future. We know God's plan for the future and it will happen. We are Light. Light reveals. Each one of us is called to reveal Him in our own special way. People can see Him in our lives, let's share Him. The miracle is that He chose us to do this.

## 32: You Share In The Heavenly Calling

*"Therefore, holy brothers, who share in the heavenly calling, fix your thoughts on Jesus, the Apostle and High Priest whom we confess" (Hebrews 3:1 NIV).*

We who share in the heavenly calling are to fix our thoughts on Jesus. Later in Hebrews we are reminded to fix our eyes and Jesus, the author and perfecter of our faith, who for the joy set before Him, endured the cross, scorning its shame, and sat down at the right hand of God. For this reason we must fix our eyes on Jesus and run the race marked out for us.

No sitting on the sidelines! No one need sit on the bench. Everyone is in the game to play and to win. Jesus has assigned us to get in there with the rest of the team. Remember, we don't do anything by ourselves. Jesus is always with us, but in addition, He surrounds us with other believers with the same goal—winning souls for the Kingdom!

And what higher calling could we have? Just the honor to be invited to participate in the salvation of another lost human being is overwhelming enough. Even more than that, working side by side with Jesus and the Holy Spirit in any endeavor takes my breath away.

Sometimes I get so excited about being involved that I forget the mission. It's like I feel Jesus and the Holy Spirit by my side and just feeling them so near me quickens my heart. I am suddenly enveloped in their presence. That's when I have to cry out, "More of you, Jesus and less of me." My prayer is that He will get my attention off myself and onto His mission. And the miracle is that you share in that Heavenly calling!

# 33:  You Are In It For The Long Haul

*"So watch your step, friends. Make sure there's no evil unbelief lying around that will trip you up and throw you off course, diverting you from the living God. For as long as it's still God's Today, keep each other on your toes so sin doesn't slow down your reflexes. If we can only keep our grip on the sure thing we started out with, we're in this with Christ for the long haul"*
*(Hebrews 3:12-14 The Message).*

You don't have to go to church to be a Christian. And on the other hand, going to church doesn't make you a Christian. But if you are a Christian, God has provided a wonderful support network through the local church. We need other believers around us to help keep us on track.

Besides the great potluck dinners and ice cream socials, church can offer small group studies and a place for you to fulfill your role in the body of Christ. At the very least, it's a place to come and get your spirit fed each week. If we're in this for the long haul, we need believing friends to see us through. Friendship takes effort so plan to find a church, make some friends in the Lord, and find ways to serve

Him.

To keep from getting tripped up on sin, make sure you're praying every day. Try to get some Bible study in, every day if you can, as often as you can. The word never wears out. God speaks to us through it constantly. His Word has a way of eliminating those nasty doubts and unbelief that can trip us. It strengthens our faith. He gave you the Manual to show you how to live and serve Him. With God, the Bible, and church, you're sure to hang in for the long haul and we'll all be united in Heaven. The miracle is that He gave us each other for the long haul!

# 34: You Are A Chosen Generation

*"But you are a chosen generation, a royal priesthood, a holy nation, His own special people, that you may proclaim the praises of Him who called you out of darkness into His marvelous light" (1 Peter 2:9 NKJV).*

The plaque on my office wall displays a famous saying from St. Francis of Assisi. He said it so well: "Lord, make an instrument of Your peace. Where there is hatred, let me sow love; where there is injury, pardon; where there is doubt, faith; where there is despair, hope; where there is darkness, light; and where there is sadness, joy."

Living up to the words on the plaque is a challenge. As one of my former pastors used to say, "Ministry isn't for wimps." I never paid much attention to that remark. I wasn't in the ministry, so it didn't apply to me. Then I came upon this verse. I read that Peter wrote this verse to Jewish Christians driven out of Jerusalem and scattered throughout Asia Minor, and to all believers everywhere.

All believers everywhere! That included me, so I went

for another look and sure enough, it says that I am a royal priesthood. In Old Testament times believers went to the priest in order to interact with God. Since Jesus delivered us from sin, He is our high priest and intercedes for us. By His authority we have been handed the priesthood. In other words, all believers have been given this great responsibility of bringing men and women to the foot of the cross.

As priests, we can go directly to Him for guidance. He will give us the tools we need. He will renew our strength both physically and mentally. Don't ever forget how valuable you are, in that the God of the universe sent His Son to die for you. Remember He loves everyone, and His greatest desire is that all will come to repentance and that none will perish.

And the miracle is this, as you bask in His glorious light, people will come to you seeking love, pardon, faith, hope, and joy. As the plaque in my office reminds me, I am God's instrument. We know the key and we can sow the seed that will give them hope and a future.

# 35: You Have Received Mercy

*"Once you were not a people, but now you are the*
*people of God; once you had not received mercy, but*
*now you have received mercy" (1 Peter 2:10 NIV).*

Being upgraded to the elevated status of a people of God
from a condemned race changes the way you think about
yourself. I know it sure did for me. I went from a sinner to
someone who knew the Word inside out. I could quote
chapter and verse to any sinner any day. I could defend
God any day of the week. After some time I guess I forgot
that I had ever been unsaved and that I was still a sinner,
saved by grace.

I began to demand perfection not only from others, but
from myself. In a flash I could spew out a Bible verse that
would cut someone down. Yes, those sinners needed to
hear the truth. Too bad if it hurt. They could get over it
and get down on their knees and confess their sins and be
saved. My holy opinion of myself kept me in the clouds
and pretty much out of touch with reality.

Then one day my whole life turned up side down. I was

at the end of my rope. God showed me mercy. I didn't deserve it, but He taught me many things through my walk through the valley of the shadow of death. One thing for sure, He taught me that He didn't need me to defend Him. He is God. Another thing He taught me was that giving mercy is as important as receiving it.

Today we can grant mercy to people all around us. It seems that everyday we run into someone who needs it. One thing about it, it doesn't cost you a red cent to do it, and if you don't extend mercy, there will spiritual repercussions.

Mercy is the closest thing to love that I can think of. And Peter said it best in 1 Peter 4:18: "Most important of all, continue to show deep love for each other, for love covers a multitude of sins" (NLT). Substitute the word mercy for love.

The miracle is that God granted you the power to generously extend mercy to anyone.

# 36: You Are A Soul-Winner

*"Friends, this world is not your home, so don't make*
*yourselves cozy in it. Don't indulge your ego at the*
*expense of your soul. Live an exemplary life among*
*the natives so that your actions will refute their*
*prejudices. Then they'll be won over to God's side and*
*be there to join the celebration when He arrives" (1*
*Peter 2:11-12 The Message).*

Over the years I suppose I have witnessed in every way
possible. At one time I walked around neighborhoods
knocking on doors and handing out tracts. Then I tried
some of what I called "guerilla witnessing." That consisted
of planting tracts in places people might see them, or
setting people up to ask about Jesus by wearing a
mysterious button on my shirt.

I've had Bible studies, attended all kinds of religious
conferences, and studied books on how to share your faith.
I traveled around the country speaking to small groups,
sharing what I learned. I have to admit that I never felt I
was very successful in any of those ventures.

Then one day I ran into a friend I hadn't seen for many years. We talked about the old neighborhood. Somehow the fact that I used to teach the neighborhood kids a Bible study came up. I didn't think much about it until she said that one of those kids was all grown up now with a family of his own. Yes, I nodded. Time does fly by.

Then she said something that took my breath away. She said she had recently seen that young man and he told her that he had accepted Christ at one of my Bible studies. There is no greater joy than knowing God has allowed you to play a part in the salvation of another. To this day I get tears in my eyes when I think about it.

And this is the miracle. God is willing to let sinners, saved by grace, participate in the most important decision someone will make in their entire life!

# 37: You Are A Threat

*"Be sober, be vigilant; because your adversary the devil walks about like a roaring lion, seeking whom he may devour" (1 Peter 5:8 NKJV).*

Ask any prominent pastor and he will tell you that the more you serve God the bigger the evil one's target is on your back. The more renowned the faithful worker for Christ, the more the evil one is threatened. God protects, for sure, but we must be mindful and in constant contact with our Lord.

Paul, that great apostle, was shipwrecked three times. He was beaten with the forty lashes minus one five times. He lived with the constant threat of death by the Jews; they looked on his conversion as treason. Three times he was beaten with rods. Once he was stoned. Why did he continue? Because sharing the gospel was worth the pain. All of the disciples, except John, suffered violent deaths. But because Jesus had already overcome death on the cross, they went to their reward. The evil one doesn't win when people die unless they are not saved.

This is why we must working and praying every day for our friends and acquaintances or people we see on the street. The counterfeiter tries to fool us into thinking he rules the world. But the world is not his and if you read the end of the book, you know that God has already won the battle. We are on God's side. We could have no more powerful leader. He will protect us. We are His hands and feet here on Earth. Serving Him is an honor and a privilege. We humbly accept the mission assigned each day.

We must be self-controlled and alert as we go about the business of serving our Lord. Evil can be very subtle. Keep your eyes open. There is no greater calling than serving our Lord. The evil one has been conquered, he has no power here on Earth. He's going down and he wants to take as many as possible with him.

And the miracle is that you are covered by the blood of Christ, and that makes you a threat to the enemy. You need not fear the enemy, but be vigilant. He will attack. Many have fallen and disgraced God's name. You can stand. God has your back.

# 38: You Are God's Child By Choice

*"What marvelous love the Father has extended to us!
Just look at it—we're called children of God! That's
who we really are. But that's also why the world
doesn't recognize us or take us seriously, because it has
no idea who He is or what He's up to" (1 John 3:1
The Message).*

At times it is inconceivable to me that the God who spoke the universe into existence loves me so much that He adopted me. That is an overwhelming fact. And then I think that He created me; and I was His in the first place. Everything belongs to Him. But He didn't want it that way.

He gave me free will so that I could decide for myself. I could have rejected Him. He wove a tapestry of my life and drew me to Him. I made a clear confession to Him, understanding that I needed to humbly repent of my sins, and He sealed me with His Holy Spirit. I feel His love all around me every day.

Our relationship could never be as intense and passionate as it is, had He just told me one day that He created me and I belonged to Him and He would control my life. Instead, He gave me the freedom to choose Him. Once the choice was made, once that decision was locked in, there was no going back. Earlier I said that when I first accepted Christ, I had no idea what I was getting into. At one point I felt like God had made a horrible mistake and that my life was a horrendous reflection on Him.

Finally I came to understand that being a child of God is a miracle of His love and grace. I get to spend a life time experiencing that love and grace every day. Most of all I get to experience Him. After all these years I still search the Scriptures to find out more about Him. I crave stories from other believers about their experiences with Him. Every day is an adventure with Him.

And the miracle is—He let you choose!

# 39: You Will Be Like Christ

*"Beloved, now we are children of God; and it has not*
*yet been revealed what we shall be, but we know that*
*when He is revealed, we shall be like Him, for we*
*shall see Him as He is" (1 John 3:2 NKJV).*

The Message puts it like this, "But friends, that's exactly who we are: children of God. And that's only the beginning. Who knows how we'll end up! What we know is that when Christ is openly revealed, we'll see Him—and in seeing Him, become like Him. All of us who look forward to His Coming stay ready, with the glistening purity of Jesus' life as a model for our own."

It seems impossible to describe this incredible relationship with God, being His child. I love the fact that it is an exciting uncertainty, this adventure with Him. We know He promises to take care of us and protect us, but we never know exactly where He is going to put us. In the same way, He promises us that one day we will be like Him and we ache for the day that happens, the day of His return.

In the meantime, we strive to be like Christ everyday. He came, not only to save us, but to teach us how to live. He painted a beautiful picture of what it is to live a sinless life. Some days we fail miserably. Those days are what I call 'learning days' because I either learn some thing that I need to change, or I am reminded that I need to lean on Abba, Father.

We really don't know what being like Christ will be. We're promised a glorified body, so we know we will have a body. We are promised to be like Him. He is eternal, beautiful, caring, comforting, compassionate, courageous, creating, distinctive, empowering, forgiving, glorified, holy, honorable, infallible, inspiring, kind, loving, perfect, powerful, protective, pure, righteous, supernatural, and victorious!

The miracle is that you will be like Him.

# 40:  You Are Safe

*"We know that anyone born of God does not continue
to sin; the One who was born of God keeps him safe,
and the evil one cannot harm him"* (1 John 5:18
*NIV).*

Now that we have a personal relationship with Jesus Christ
we are perfect and never sin. No! That is far from the truth.
The truth is that believers sometimes fail in their attempts
to be more like Him. Sometimes we get angry when we
shouldn't. Sometimes we backslide. Sometimes we just miss
the mark.

What makes us different from the rest of the world is
that we can go to the Father through Jesus, repent and
confess our sin, and ask for forgiveness. God forgives us
and we can leave that sin behind. It frees us to pick up
where we left off in serving our Lord. No, Christians are
not perfect, but they are forgiven.

We live in a world where we are confronted by sin every
day. We go about our business during the day and drive
past advertisements that shouldn't even be on the

highways. We go shopping and as we check out we see gossip magazines on the stand addressing all the messy personal issues of famous people that are idolized, then we got home and turn on the TV to watch the news only to see advertisements that push premarital sex and immorality of all kinds.

It is God's will that we live in this world without sin. We are confronted by it all the time, but Jesus promised to bring us through. The very fact that He was tempted in the wilderness for forty days gives us the assurance that He knows what we deal with every day.

The evil one has been defeated at Calvary. He has no power over us. He cannot make you do anything. One of my favorite Scriptures is "resist the devil and he will flee" (James 4:7). This is so practical when you are tempted. Resist the devil. In the name of Jesus command him to leave you alone and fill your thoughts with Christ. It works. He leaves. Perhaps for ten seconds, perhaps for one day, or until you let your guard down; but the devil flees. He wants no part of praising Jesus. The miracle is that nothing can stop you from praising the Lord!

# About the Author

Vicki and her husband, David, live in Erie, Colorado. She received her bachelor's degree from Belleview Bible College, Westminster, Colorado. Her Master's thesis, *History of the Relationship between the United States and Israel,* merited Magna Cum Laude honors. She earned her doctorate in Practical Theology in Biblical Counseling from Master's Graduate School of Divinity, Evansville, Indiana.

Vicki wrote about her experiences in Jerusalem in her first book, *On Our Own in Jerusalem's Old City—Two Born-Again Christians Explore Their Hebraic Roots.* For the next three years she wrote a fictional account of a wealthy Jewish family in *The Lane Trilogy— Lyza's Story, The Legacy,* and *Leesa's Story.*

Vicki continues to write Christian inspirational books, both fiction and non-fiction. She speaks at all types of events to educate, motivate and elevate Christian women everywhere. Her messages have been distributed through radio, television, YouTube, Facebook, and Twitter.

Made in the USA
San Bernardino, CA
23 September 2014